Jack and the Beanstalk

Retold and dramatised as a reading play
for partners or small groups.

Ways to read this story

This story is suitable for school and home. Some 'how to read' ideas are below.

- With a partner or small group, take it in turns to read the rows.

- Don't rush! This helps you to say each word clearly.

- Think of yourselves as actors by adding lots of facial and vocal expression. Small gaps of silence also create dramatic energy. These techniques will bring the story to life.

- If you meet a new word, try to break it down and then say it again. If you have any problems, ask your teacher or a reading buddy.

- Don't be scared of unusual words. They will become your new best friends. (New words strengthen your general knowledge and enable you to become vocabulary-rich in your day-to-day life.)

There was once a poor widow who had a son called Jack.

Jack and his mother lived in a little cottage in the countryside, not far from a small town.

Every morning just as the sun was rising, Jack would go out into the crisp morning air to where their dairy cow Milky White was waiting to be milked.

Without fail, Milky White always gave Jack a bucket full of beautiful rich creamy milk.

He would then put the bucket of milk into the cool pantry on the other side of the house.

By midday each day, the cream had risen to the top of the milk, which Jack and his mother then scooped off to turn into rich butter to sell.

Early one spring morning just after Jack went out to do the milking as usual, he called out to his mother in a very worried voice.

'Mother! Mother! I think there's a big problem with Milky White.'

'What sort of problem, Jack? What's wrong?'

'Milky White has no more milk. That means we can't make butter because we don't have milk.'

'Oh dear. We must have a milking cow if we are to survive. Milky White has to be sold.'

'Sell Milky White! Oh no! I love the way she moos softly in the morning when I come out to milk her. Maybe she'll be alright tomorrow!'

'No, Jack. We have to be strong. Take her to the town market today. Off you go before I become too upset!'

And so after breakfast, off trudged Jack towards the town, Milky White walking slowly beside him.

'Well, hello, Jack! Where are you and Milky White off to on such a fine morning?'

A funny little man in a green suit and a red velvet hat was standing at the side of the road.

'Good morning, sir. I am going to the town market to sell my cow. But may I please ask how you know our names?'

'I know everyone's name just by looking at them. I now need to ask you a serious question if I may.'

'Why you are selling Milky White after all the years of service she has given you?'

'I don't want to sell her, but she has run dry. My mother and I need a cow that will give us lots of rich creamy milk.'

'I like the look of Milky White, Jack m' lad, and I think I have the perfect place where she could have a happy retirement.'

'Well, sir, I will only sell her to someone who will keep her safe and happy.'

'A good answer, young Jack. If I buy her, she'll spend her days eating fresh grass and sleeping in the sunshine. And I will pay you handsomely.'

'That's a very tempting offer, sir, but exactly how much are you willing to pay?'

'I will give you something much better than money, young Jack. This little bag has more treasure in it than you can ever imagine!'

'Oh thank you, sir. My mother *will* be pleased, but is it enough to buy a new milking cow and perhaps a second-hand sewing machine?'

'More than enough for a herd of cows and the best sewing machine in the world, Master Jack.'

'A herd of cows *and* a sewing machine?'

'Both are within reach, young Jack. But please think carefully before you make your decision.'

'Mmm. My mother loves to sew, and we certainly need a new cow. Yes, I will shake hands on it.'

'Done, Master Jack! Here is your treasure.'

'And here is Milky White.'

'Now close your eyes and count to twenty. That will start the magic of the treasure.'

So Jack closed his eyes and counted slowly.

'… eighteen, nineteen, twenty.'

When Jack opened his eyes to wish them good luck, they had already disappeared.

Jack ran home as fast as the wind.

'Mother, mother! Good news! A funny little man gave me a bag of treasure in exchange for Milky White.'

'Oh, well done, my clever son! Treasure, you say? Perhaps it's a pair of silver dollars!'

'He said it is enough to buy lots of cows, dear Mother, and the best sewing machine in …'

But as soon as Jack's mother opened the little bag, all her dreams went crashing to the floor.

Her screams were so loud that Jack's mouth went dry and his face turned pale.

'Oh Mother! I am so sorry.'

'Beans! I thought this was a bag of treasure! Now we don't even own a dry cow – and we certainly can't buy a sewing machine with beans!'

'But the man said there would be enough …'

'Out the window go these silly beans.'

'And you, Jack, can go straight to bed for the rest of the day. How could you treat your poor dear mother like this?'

And so out the window went the beans, and upstairs to bed went Jack.

During the night, strange things started to happen in the garden.

Strong little shoots sprouted out from the beans, and roots pushed themselves down into the soil.

Instead of bright yellow sunshine waking Jack next morning, a pale green light shone through the bedroom window. Something odd had happened.

Jack jumped out of bed, dressed quickly, and ran downstairs and into the garden.

'Oh me, oh my! Those beans must have been special after all! How else could they grow into such a *huge* beanstalk?'

'I wonder how far up it goes ... Well, there is only one way to find out.'

And so Jack started climbing. The beanstalk branches were in just the right places for his feet.

The higher Jack climbed, the taller the beanstalk seemed to go.

The beanstalk eventually stopped in a very thick cloud. Jack jumped off and had a look around.

'What now? I need to think about this. Where do I go from here?'

'Just a minute. How odd! A pathway has just appeared near my feet.'

'It leads to a huge castle over there in the distance, so that's where I'll go. I wonder if there will be anyone at home.'

So off Jack went across the clouds.

He followed the path until he arrived at a very large green wooden door.

He was wondering what to say if he was asked why he was visiting so early in the morning, when the big green door opened.

A tall woman with a kind face looked down at him.

'My goodness! A visitor! And a smart-looking young lad if ever I saw one. Who are you, and what do you want, young man?'

'My name is Jack, and I – I would like to ask if you have, um, any breakfast to spare. Would you perhaps have a piece of leftover toast?'

'Leftover toast! Ha! You'll be spread on a piece of toast if the giant finds you on his doorstep. You'd better come inside quickly before he ...'

But there was no time for the woman to finish her sentence. Everything started to shake.

'Hurry! Get yourself in here and out of the way. It's my husband, the giant!'

'A giant! Where can I hide, Mrs Giant? Your husband doesn't sound at all friendly.'

'He's probably in a bad mood because he forgot to have his tank of tea this morning.'

'Jump into this cold oven, young man. You'll be as safe as houses in here!'

And so Jack jumped into the cold oven with just the barest of moments to spare.

Through the thick oven door, Jack could hear the heavy footsteps of the giant getting closer.

Suddenly, a low, deep voice shouted out like a volcano erupting.

'Fe-fi-fi-fo-fum,
I smell the blood of an Englishman.
Be he alive or be he dead
I'll grind his bones to make my bread.
If he's tall or if he's short
It won't be long before he's caught!'

Luckily, the giant's wife knew what to say.

'I don't know what you mean, dear. There's no-one here. Look around for yourself.'

'But I smell something, and this great big nose of mine never lets me down!'

'It's probably the twenty rashes of bacon, a dozen tomatoes and fifteen extra-large eggs that I'm cooking for you that you can smell, husband dear!'

And Jack heard the giant's wife bang a few saucepans and give a happy laugh. The giant grunted a few times and then went off to wash his hands, his footsteps fading into the distance.

The door of the oven snapped open. The giant's wife peered in and whispered urgently to Jack.

'After breakfast the giant always counts his gold and tells his poor little goose to lay yet another golden egg for his collection.'

'And then he falls asleep. That's when you can make your escape.'

And the oven door snapped shut once more.

Jack knew he would have to hide for quite a long while, so he settled himself down as comfortably as he could.

He was able to tell what was happening by the sounds he heard.

First, the loud footsteps returned to the kitchen.

A chair scraped on the floor.

A tank of tea was slurped.

Cutlery was clattered.

Toast was crunched.

After plates were collected, Jack heard coins clinking and numbers being mumbled.

Grunts and bad counting came in between these mumbles, and Jack grinned to himself.

After what seemed to be hours, Jack at last heard loud snoring in the distance.

The oven door opened once again. The giant's wife spoke to Jack in a loud whisper.

'Jack, my dear! The coast is clear. The giant is asleep in the sunroom. Here is some toast and honey, you poor starving boy. Now tell me something – why are you here?'

'My mother is very worried because our cow went dry, and we have no money to buy food, and everything is going wrong.'

'Not enough money for food! That is terrible! Your mother will be at her wits' end. She'll also be wondering where on earth you are.'

'I insist you take this bag of gold and this goose to your mother. I will tell the giant that his goose flew away and that I needed the bag of gold in my workshop.'

'Goodbye and good luck, young Jack. Now quickly. Run like the wind!'

Jack thanked the giant's wife, and holding the bag of gold and the goose, he sped along the path until he came to the top of the beanstalk.

Down he climbed, carefully carrying the gifts for his mother as he went.

As soon as Jack's feet touched the ground of home, he called out in his loudest voice.

'Mother! Mother! Look what I have! You'll never believe what has happened.'

Jack's mother came rushing out of the house, drying her hands on her apron as she ran. She had a worried look on her face.

'Where have you been, my precious boy? I'm so sorry I was cross with you last night. I know that you were only trying to do your best for us both.'

'You will never believe the adventure I've had, Mother.'

'At the top of the beanstalk there was a huge castle, and a friendly lady called Mrs Giant lived there with her really grumpy giant husband.'

'Mrs Giant gave me these presents to give to you, Mother dear. Open your arms wide!'

'Oh my goodness, Jack. I can't believe it! A truly beautiful goose and a bag of gold coins. This is treasure indeed!'

'We will be able to buy a whole herd of cows and a sewing machine as well. And at last I'll be able to make ballgowns for fine ladies.'

And that's exactly what happened.

From the herd of cows there was so much rich creamy milk that Jack and his mother were able to not only make butter, but cheese as well.

Jack's mother saved enough money to buy beautiful satins, silks, ribbons and laces which she turned into magnificent ballgowns using her new sewing machine.

A year or so later, and just before his sixteenth birthday, Jack decided to climb the beanstalk once more. He wanted to tell the giant's wife how well things were going.

Mrs Giant beamed with pleasure to hear about the butter, the cheese-making and the sewing machine. But then she had another idea.

'Jack, young man. The giant makes his golden harp play the same old, same old music twenty-four seven, and it totally gets on my nerves.'

'So here is my plan. I think the harp would love to have a new owner so that it can play lots of different tunes. Please take it and give it to your mother as a gift.'

'Why thank you, Mrs Giant. But what will your husband say when he finds his harp missing?'

'I will take care of that, dear Jack. Now off you go. Run like the wind, and please give my very best wishes to your mother!'

Jack raced through the castle corridors faster than he had ever run before to make his escape. Suddenly, a voice boomed out …

'Fe-fi-fi-fo-fum
I smell the blood of an Englishman.
Be he alive, or be he dead,
I'll grind his bones to make my bread
If he's tall or if he's short,
It won't be long before …'

But Jack didn't listen to the giant's words.

His thoughts were only on how to escape! The topmost branches of the beanstalk magically appeared in front of his feet.
As fast as possible, Jack started his descent.

However, with his long strides, the giant didn't take long to also reach the top of the beanstalk.

The leaves shook and swayed as the giant's large boots found footholds on the branches. Down he went, shouting out loudly at the same time.

'Come back here with my golden harp, you young scallywag.'

Jack had almost reached the ground when he saw his mother come running out of the house.

'Mother, Mother! The giant is coming down the beanstalk, and he wants to catch me!'

'Quickly! Take this harp and hide it in the house. Hurry! There's no time to lose!'

Jack's mother put the harp under a bed before hurrying back to where Jack was standing.

The beanstalk shuddered with the weight of the giant as he climbed further and further down.

And then suddenly, the beanstalk stopped shuddering.

Far up above, Jack and his mother could hear some grunting noises and then a voice talking to itself.

'A beanstalk is not a safe place for a giant. And, I can smell lunch cooking back home in my castle.'

'I'm definitely starving to bits. And I've decided that stalks of any kind are far too dangerous for a handsome chap like me to climb.'

'Ah yes. Definitely much too dangerous!'

'And if I'm honest with myself – I'm a bit tired of hearing harp music every single day.'

'So – if that young lad wants a second-hand harp, he's more than welcome to it!'

And so the giant climbed back up the beanstalk.

When he returned to the castle he saw that his wife had prepared a magnificent lunch for them both – sixteen hamburgers with the works for him, and ten vegetarian salads for her.

For dessert they shared a chocolate mud cake and a tub of icecream.
Over coffee, the giant's wife presented her husband with two golden boxes encrusted with precious jewels.

She had only just finished making them in her castle workroom that very morning, and now they sparkled and glistened like the midday sun.

'What have we here, my sweet one? Have you been busy in your workshop again?'

And the giant exclaimed with loud cries of delight and happiness as he unwrapped each box.

'A-*ha*! You have replaced my old harp with a music box that reads stories and sings songs.'

'But only in the mornings, dear husband.'

'And what else have you made? Oh yes! What I've always wanted – an electronic chess set!'

'But it only works in the afternoons, dear husband, only in the afternoons!'

'That means that we can walk among the clouds in the evenings and watch the stars appear. I will never be bored again. Thank you, clever wife.'

Meanwhile, the goose lived out her days happily foraging among flowers in every colour of the rainbow that grew in the Jack's mother's garden.

Every now and again she laid a golden egg in a rose-petal nest to prove she still had magic powers.

The harp occasionally played a snappy tune as a surprise on quiet evenings, but only if there was a full moon and a clear sky.

Mysteriously, the beanstalk completely vanished one cold rainy morning and never grew again.

A few years later, Jack built his mother a sewing room, and she made magnificent satin ballgowns for queens and princesses all over the world.

Jack became a famous cheese maker. He married his childhood sweetheart, and they built a house of their own nearby with lots of bedrooms for their children.

The children often asked their mother, father or grandma to tell them their favourite bedtime story because they loved it so much.

This favourite story had some magic powers of its own because although the main events stayed the same, the details often changed, so there were always surprises.

And if you haven't guessed already, the name of this favourite story was, of course …

… Jack and the Beanstalk!